OH, THE STORIES YOU WILL WRITE: THE WORKBOOK

OH, THE STORIES YOU WILL WRITE: THE WORKBOOK

STEFANI MILAN

Milan Book Publishing

Copyright © 2023 by Stefani Milan

Published by Milan Book Publishing in 2023.

All rights reserved. No part of this book may be reproduced in any manner whatsoever without written permission except in the case of brief quotations embodied in critical articles and reviews. Photocopy permission is granted for personal use only. For other inquiries, please get in touch with the publisher at admin@milanbookpublishing.com.

First Printing, 2023
Milan Book Publishing
NJ, USA

CONTENTS

About This Workbook   vii

1
EXERCISES TO JUMP-START YOUR WRITING!   1

Writing Exercise Day #1: Imagination Run Wild   3

Writing Exercise Day #2: Goodbye, Good Riddance   5

Writing Exercise Day #3: Excuses Begone!   9

Writing Exercise Day #4: Please Come To A Full And Complete Stop   13

Writing Exercise Day #5: Leap And Achieve   17

Writing Exercise Day #6: Set Your Intention For Writing   19

Writing Exercise Day #7: Word Loggin'   23

Writing Exercise Day #8: Writing Goals   27

Writing Exercise Day #9: Basic Character Blueprint   31

Writing Exercise Day #10: Determine Your Creative Space   35

Writing Exercise Day #11: Determine Your Writing Style   39

Writing Exercise Day #12: Your Ideal Writing Tribe   41

Writing Exercise Day #13: Music Memory   43

Writing Exercise Day #14: Volcano Of Creativity   45

Writing Exercise Day #15: Book Cover Brain Trick   49

Writing Exercise Day #16: Engaging The Senses   53

Writing Exercise Day #17: What's The Buzz?   55

Writing Exercise Day #18: Current Status: Critical   57

Writing Exercise Day #19: Loveth Thy Selfeth   59

Writing Exercise Day #20: Call The Clutter Man!   63

Writing Exercise Day #21: Empower Yourself   67

2
A DEEPER DIVE INTO DEVELOPING YOUR BOOK — **71**

Bestseller Mapping Exercise Day #1: Getting Started — 73

Bestseller Mapping Exercise Day #2: Let's Set The Scene — 75

Bestseller Mapping Exercise Day #3: Diving Deeper — 76

Bestseller Mapping Exercise Day #4: Getting To The Finish Line — 78

Bestseller Mapping Exercise Day #5: Applying This Process To Your Work — 80

Keypoints About Mapping A Bestseller — 82

3
WORKSHEETS TO KEEP WRITING MOMENTUM — **83**

Word Goal Log — 85

Small Writing Goal To-Do List — 87

Twelve Tips For Writing Success — 89

The Empowered Mindset — 91

A Guide To Confidence Building — 92

Final Thoughts — 93
Acknowledgments — 95
About The Author — 96
More By Milan Book Publishing — 97

ABOUT THIS WORKBOOK

This workbook is designed to accompany the book, *Oh, the Stories You Will Write: A Motivational Guide to Empower Aspiring Authors*. As I stated in *Oh, the Stories You Will Write*, when I first wrote a book on creativity, I did not realize how many people had a desire to write a book. I love coaching aspiring authors, but I wanted a way to reach more people and bring them proven exercises to ignite a fire within them and keep them motivated on their writing journeys. That is the main purpose of this workbook.

To me, any desire is like a seed; the more we water and nurture it, the more it will grow. In this way, you, as a "budding author" will grow as you water and nurture your writing desires and skills. I have always believed that if a person puts his mind to something, he will achieve his goal. In this workbook, you'll find exercises that will act as water and food for that seed of desire.

In **Part One**, you'll find twenty-one days of journal exercises that will help to keep building momentum toward your writing goals.

In **Part Two**, you'll take a deeper dive into building writing skills and keeping your writing momentum flowing in the right direction with "mapping a bestseller" exercises.

In **Part Three**, you'll find worksheets that, with the purchase of this workbook, you are granted permission to copy and keep with you daily, not just for this book you are writing, but for the books you will write in the future. You will also find both the **Empowered Mindset** list and **A Guide to Confidence Building** list from *Oh, the Stories You Will Write*, which you can turn to whenever you feel you have steered off course. Lastly, you'll find my **Ten Tips for Success** that you can refer to whenever needed.

Throughout the workbook, you will find quotes from *Oh, the Stories You Will Write* to keep you motivated along the way.

What I love about this workbook is that you can use these exercises over and over again for each book you write. Eventually, you'll establish your own writing routine and style that will bring you joy and help you complete your books.

Even though I may not personally be there coaching you, please know I am there with you energetically on your journey, cheering for you to write and complete the book you have always wanted to write.

Never forget that your desire is the seed, and as you water and nurture this desire, you will be amazed at what will grow!

All my best to you,

Stefani

1

Exercises to Jump-Start Your Writing!

Writing Exercise Day #1: Imagination Run Wild

"Once we begin to build momentum toward our dreams, one day we will look back in amazement at how far we've come."

CHAPTER ONE
OH, THE STORIES YOU WILL WRITE

Writing Exercise #1: Imagination Run Wild

In Chapter One of *Oh, the Stories You Will Write,* I talk about the power of momentum and how that helps us write and finish our books. In this exercise, you are going to imagine your life as though you changed your current momentum or increased it and began to follow your dream. What does it feel like? What does it look like? Visualize what your life is like now that you have no excuses and have jumped out of your comfort zone and into the unknown. See yourself taking action towards writing a book every day. Visualize it published. Where do you live? How many books are you selling? How many books are you publishing? Are you editor-in-chief of a big magazine or a big publishing company? Do you own your own publishing company? Whatever your dream is, envision it, but most importantly, envision yourself HAPPILY doing it.

_____
_____
_____
_____
_____
_____
_____
_____
_____
_____
_____
_____
_____
_____
_____
_____
_____
_____
_____
_____
_____
_____

Writing Exercise Day #2: Goodbye, Good Riddance

"We must find ways to achieve our true purpose and passion. The fulfillment we experience from this pursuit allows us to experience a pure form of happiness. The way in which we achieve this dream may be different from what we originally thought, but nevertheless achieving our dream is always possible, no matter what our circumstances are."

CHAPTER ONE
OH, THE STORIES YOU WILL WRITE

Writing Exercise #2: Goodbye, Good Riddance

Think about the limiting beliefs you learned over the years and accepted as truths. What have your parents, teachers, siblings, friends, and clergy said about:

Following your dreams? (Examples: *The business is too difficult. You have to pay your dues to achieve your dreams. You're too old to start a new career. You need to have more credentials to do that. You can only achieve your dream through struggle...*)

Earning Money? (Examples: *The economy is bad. Rich people are bad. Money doesn't grow on trees. Money isn't everything.*)

Self-esteem (Examples: *I'm overweight. I'm not good enough. I'm not smart enough. I'm too old. I'm too young. I'm not skilled enough.*)

The list goes on and on for some people. Write every limiting belief down. But remember to not blame or be angry with those who may have conditioned you with a limiting belief. After all, you have accepted this belief as true, and you have the power to UN-accept it. Defriend it. Block it. Make a commitment to release all of your limiting beliefs and create a new mindset of your own.

Affirm: *(Insert limiting belief) no longer holds power over me. I am releasing it forever, and I am replacing it with a better and more positive belief that is my own belief and no one else's. I understand that those who conditioned me before were doing the best they could, and I forgive them now. I no longer accept beliefs as true unless they elevate me and others.*

Current limiting belief someone said:
_____

New, positive belief:
_____

Current limiting belief someone said:
_____

New, positive belief:

_____

Current limiting belief someone said:
_____

New, positive belief:

_____

Current limiting belief someone said:
_____

New, positive belief:

_____

Current limiting belief someone said:
_____

New, positive belief:

_____

Writing Exercise Day #3: Excuses Begone!

"If you have a dream to write a book, then you must leap into that unknown and write the book. Hesitation does not bring you closer to your goal. Only leaps, failures, and improvements will do that."

CHAPTER TWO
OH, THE STORIES YOU WILL WRITE

Writing Exercise #3: Excuses Begone!

This exercise is similar to the last exercise, except that instead of focusing on what *other* people have said to us, we are focusing on what we say to ourselves. Negative statements we tell ourselves become excuses for not completing what we wish to finish (in this case, not writing that book we have always wanted to write)! In the first part of this exercise, write down any excuses you have made about why you cannot complete or follow your dream of writing a book or any other dream. Then, write a power statement that overrides that excuse. See the example below.

Example:
Excuse: I do not have time to write a book.
Power statement: I make time each day to write.

Excuse #1

_____

Excuse #2

_____

Excuse #3

_____

Excuse #4

_____

Excuse #5

_____

Now, let's flip those excuses into power statements about what we know we can achieve! Be sure to catch yourself in the future any time you are making an excuse. Again, the key to changing habits is to be aware.

Power Statement #1

_____

Power Statement #2

_____

Power Statement #3

_____

Power Statement #4

_____

Power Statement #5

_____

How do you feel when you repeat your power statement compared to your excuse?

_____
_____
_____

Remember to repeat your power statements every day!

Writing Exercise Day #4: Please Come to a Full and Complete Stop

"Because we are in control of our thoughts, we have the ability to change our habits and circumstances by changing our thoughts."

CHAPTER ONE
OH, THE STORIES YOU WILL WRITE

Writing Exercise #4: Please Come to a Full and Complete Stop

Think about some habits you currently have that you would like to change. Write them down. **Remember to please slow the car down and come to a full and complete stop before building a new momentum or habit in a new direction. (Otherwise, you're going to be very, very dizzy.)** Once you have identified the habits you would like to change, write down the new habit you would like to create.

Every day say, *"This habit of (insert habit) is driving my momentum in the wrong direction. This habit no longer serves me. I am aware of this habit and am taking one step today to cultivate the new habit of (insert the habit you would like to create). Each day I am building this new habit that is leading me toward happiness and fulfillment."*

Do not punish yourself or get angry if you repeat the same habit even after you told yourself you are going to change. The key is to be aware of the thought or habit and affirm that you are aware of it. The more aware you are of the habit, the easier it will be to change.

Current habit:
_____

Desired habit:
_____

Current habit:
_____

Desired habit:
_____

Current habit: _____

Desired habit: _____

Writing Exercise Day #5: Leap and Achieve

"Leapers take chances. They leap with big dreams and virtually no strategies. They see an end goal and do not look before they leap into the unknown of their dreams. Hesitators, on the other hand, may never leap toward their dreams. They wait for the right circumstances, opportunities, skills, and people to make their move."

CHAPTER TWO
OH, THE STORIES YOU WILL WRITE

Writing Exercise #5: Leap and Achieve

Are you a leaper or a hesitator? Are there situations in your life where you wish you had "taken the chance?" While we cannot change the past, we can make positive changes in our future. Name a current dream or circumstance where you could become a "leaper."

_____
_____
_____
_____
_____
_____
_____
_____
_____
_____
_____
_____
_____
_____
_____
_____
_____
_____
_____
_____
_____
_____

Writing Exercise Day #6: Set Your Intention for Writing

"The stronger your intention is for writing, the stronger your attention will be to your goal and the easier it will be to write your story."

CHAPTER THREE
OH, THE STORIES YOU WILL WRITE

Writing Exercise #6: Set Your Intention for Writing

Let's answer the most important question.

1. Why do you want to write a book? In Chapter Three of *Oh, the Stories You Will Write*, I discuss why having a "Strong Output Intention (S.O.I.)" is crucial to finishing your book! As I stated in the book, the stronger your *intention* is for writing a book, the stronger the *attention* you will give to completing it. So, what are your reasons for wanting to write a book in the first place?

_____
_____
_____
_____
_____
_____
_____
_____
_____
_____
_____
_____

Now, see if you can create an even stronger intention. (If you can't, that's okay!)

_____
_____
_____
_____
_____
_____
_____
_____
_____
_____
_____
_____

As you grow comfortable with "why" you want to write your book, begin to share your intentions with others that you **know will support your dreams**. The encouragement from *supportive* people will generate more excitement for you.

Just a note. Sometimes we will excitedly share our dreams with people who we want to be happy for us, but who are unhappy with themselves and appear unsupportive. Do not dismay! Simply stop sharing your dreams with them and pursue your dream anyway! Regardless of whether or not people are supportive of your writing dreams, ***you are the only one who can truly make them happen***, so you must rely on your own confidence and strong intentions instead of other people's opinions.

2. What is your book idea? Write a short paragraph explaining the book you always wanted to write. You may have several, but for this exercise, let's focus on one.

_____
_____
_____
_____
_____
_____
_____
_____
_____
_____
_____
_____
_____
_____
_____
_____
_____
_____
_____
_____
_____

Writing Exercise Day #7: Word Loggin'

"The key to success with word goals is to start small...300-500 words a day for beginners is a good place to start with word goals."

CHAPTER FOUR
OH, THE STORIES YOU WILL WRITE

Writing Exercise #7: Word Loggin'

Word Log: Set a short-term word goal and create a word-goal chart. I've included an example below, but you can find a Word Log Chart at the end of this workbook. For new writers, I suggest a goal of 300 words a day for 15 minutes. Increase your goals as you build more writing momentum.

Note: Even if you do not reach your goal, log in how many words you did write.

Day/Date	Word Goal	Words Written	Writing Time
Monday	300	500	15 mins
Tuesday	400	400	30 mins
Wednesday	400	200	10mins
Thursday	400	1000	1hr.
Friday	300	0	0
Saturday	400	800	1.5hrs

Let's come up with a short word goal now, between 100-500 words.

_____

Word Goal Log

As you can see from the chart on the previous page, your chart may vary. It is the consistency of filling out the chart and mostly hitting your mark with your word goals that will build momentum and help you reach your goals. Now you try it!

Day/Date	Word Goal	Words Written	Writing Time
Monday			
Tuesday			
Thursday			
Friday			
Saturday			

Remember to start small.

Writing Exercise Day #8: Writing Goals

"A small writing goal might be to complete one scene or chapter or finish a part of your outline. You might even work on one paragraph. Small writing goals are personal and will depend on how much you feel you can accomplish on a particular day, but try to keep it small. Set yourself up for writing success."

CHAPTER FOUR
OH, THE STORIES YOU WILL WRITE

Writing Exercise #8: Writing Goals

In this section, we are going to focus on both long-term and short-term writing goals. Let's begin with long-term goals!

1. Long-Term Writing Goals

For these goals, we must ask ourselves where do we see ourselves as writers six months from now? One year from now? Five years from now? Ten years from now?

It is important for us to write these goals down where we can look at them every day. Examples may be:

Six months: *Halfway finished first novel.*
One year: *Completed first novel. Working on publishing.*
Five year: *Sequel to first novel completed and published; New series first book completed and published.*
Ten year: *Over ten books completed and published.*

Six month goal:
_____

One year goal:
_____

Five year goal:
_____

Ten year goal:
_____

2. **Small Writing Goals:** For the remainder of this workbook, we will create "small" writing goals for each week. Small writing goals help us to build momentum without overwhelming ourselves.

A **Small Writing Goal Chart** is included in this workbook that you have permission to copy and use on your writing journey. For now, set a small writing goal to help you begin writing the book you always wanted to write. Perhaps you would like to focus on a character that has been speaking to you or a particular scene you have been playing repeatedly in your mind. Maybe you have had an experience that you would like to write about. Pick one small goal you feel you can commit to writing about that pertains to your book idea, and write that small goal below. For now, you're just setting the goal. We will work on applying our goals in future exercises.

I commit to writing about
_____
_____
_____
_____
_____
_____
_____
_____

Writing Exercise Day #9: Basic Character Blueprint

"Character blueprints are like the basic sketches an artist might make of a human body or what an architect might draft for a house or building plan. These blueprints are certainly not the final product, but they serve as an outline for why our characters may behave the way they do."

CHAPTER FOUR
OH, THE STORIES YOU WILL WRITE

Writing Exercise #9: Basic Character Blueprint

For this small writing goal exercise, you can either work with a character you have been developing or one you have always wanted to write. You can also start from scratch. Using the character blueprint section from *Oh, the Stories You Will Write*, or on your own, come up with a basic outline of who your character is.

Start by creating his "bookends." Who is this character right now? Is he good? Loyal? Evil? Untrustworthy? Afraid? Altruistic? Who this character is right now forms one end of his bookends. Now, think about his childhood. Who was this person as a child? How did he grow up? Where? What was the environment in which he grew up? What circumstances did he face? What kind of subconscious programming did he receive that may be playing out in his adult life? (You do not need to create an adult character for this section, of course.) Now, list any teen or adult experiences that may change or enhance his childhood programming. As an example, let's say he grew up in a happy home but as a young adult experiences a tremendous loss. How might that affect him?

Questions to think about:
What are your character's strengths?
What are your character's flaws?
What feminine energies does he exhibit (compassion, strength through emotion and communication, gentleness, warmth, empathy, imagination, etc.)?
What masculine energies does he exhibit (physical strength, bravery, leadership, assertiveness, logic and reasoning, confidence, integrity, etc.)?
What societal conditioning does he fall into (ex: competition instead of cooperation)?
What beliefs are strong for him (political, religious, etc.)?

This blueprint can take time to create. You might even need to step away and then return to developing this character. If you are using a real person for your blueprint (especially useful if you are writing a memoir) then you might even begin to understand the reason for this person's behavior over the years.

_____
_____
_____
_____
_____
_____

Writing Exercise Day #10: Determine Your Creative Space

"Finding a special writing place or atmosphere is another way we can access untapped creativity and focus our energy on writing and completing a book or writing project."

CHAPTER FIVE
OH, THE STORIES YOU WILL WRITE

Writing Exercise #10: Determine Your Creative Space

Your small writing goal for today is to determine which atmosphere makes you feel most productive by bringing your journal or laptop to a café or any other crowded space and trying to free-write. If this space is too noisy, try a quieter room in your house or someplace you know you won't be disturbed. Which writing space makes you feel comfortable and stimulates your creativity? Try writing in different places and examine how each atmosphere makes you feel in order to determine your favorite writing space. Keep a log of your experiences in the space below.

Writing Exercise Day #11: Determine Your Writing Style

"Try all the writing styles and see what feels right to you!"

CHAPTER FIVE
OH, THE STORIES YOU WILL WRITE

Writing Exercise #11: Determine Your Writing Style

Your small goal for today is to take one idea you have always wanted to write about and try to create a scene using the outline or storyboard writing style. Draw pictures, similar to a graphic novel style, or simply list the events that happen in the scene from start to finish. If all else fails, simply free-write the scene. Determine which process makes you feel most productive.

Writing Exercise Day #12: Your Ideal Writing Tribe

"The reason aligning with people who have the same energy as you do about writing is important (especially if you are optimistic and excited about your writing career) is that with your "tribe," you will feel uplifted, more determined, and eager to continue your writing rather than feeling defeated, exhausted, and insecure about your next steps."

CHAPTER FIVE
OH, THE STORIES YOU WILL WRITE

Writing Exercise #12: Your Ideal Writing Tribe

Let's use our imaginations now to create our ideal writing tribe. If you had a group of three or four writers in your writing group, what kind of people would they be? Would they be authors who only traditionally publish or those that are into self-publishing? Would they be seasoned writers or beginners? What type of energy would they have? Would they be happy and excited people? Quiet? Would they keep to themselves? Would your group be relaxed and laid back or more professional and reserved?

This is an imaginary list unless you already have a writing group. Everyone in the group is going to have strengths and weaknesses. What makes the tribe powerful is when each member contributes his own unique strengths. Remember to be wary of those with negative mindsets as this can severely impact your progress as a writer.

1. Name (can be made up or someone you know that you would love to have in your group)
2. Why are they part of your writing tribe?
3. How reliable are they?
4. What are their writing strengths that you admire?
5. What are their writing weaknesses (someone else in your writing tribe may have this as a strength and other weaknesses)?
6. Do they reciprocate assistance the way that you do?
7. How can you participate better with this person?
8. What skills do you possess that will enhance the group as a whole?

_____
_____
_____
_____
_____
_____
_____
_____
_____
_____
_____
_____

Writing Exercise Day #13: Music Memory

"Music helps us feel our emotions, and when we are writing, we want to access our deepest emotions for our characters so they may grow."

CHAPTER SIX
OH, THE STORIES YOU WILL WRITE

Writing Exercise #13: Music Memory

Think of a song that had a profound impact on you. Close your eyes and listen to it. Think of why that song had an impact on you. Whatever the situation, in the space below, write down how that song affected you using your senses as you listen to the song. (*I suggest a song that is not too emotionally draining, as the point of the exercise is to stimulate the senses but not drain our emotions.*)

1. How do you feel when you hear the song?
2. What types of people, places, or things do you see in your mind as you listen?
3. If you remember a specific time period as you listen, think of what other sounds you heard at the time.
4. Do you remember smells? Aromas of delicious food or terrible odors?
5. Were you touching anything? Holding on to a precious gift? Letting something go?
6. Did you taste anything during the song? Perhaps you were eating dinner, a treat, or fine dining at a wedding or restaurant. Maybe you were drinking a beer or a cold glass of iced tea.

Now, look at your descriptions and listen to the song again, putting all the sights and sounds together in your mind. Does the memory come alive? Music has the capacity to do this for us.

_____
_____
_____
_____
_____
_____
_____
_____
_____
_____
_____
_____
_____
_____
_____
_____
_____
_____
_____
_____
_____
_____
_

Writing Exercise Day #14: Volcano of Creativity

"Because music touches our hearts so profoundly, it is very useful in helping us write rich plots and characters. Through the use of music, while writing, we can unleash boundless creativity."

CHAPTER SIX
OH, THE STORIES YOU WILL WRITE

Writing Exercise #14: Volcano of Creativity

Whatever it is you want to write about, there is a song that is ready and willing to help stimulate your imagination. For this exercise, we are actually going to write a scene. To begin, pick any one of the following examples to write about.

1. An old man walked down the street with a cane...
2. A young, beautiful woman stood at the top of a hill...
3. A frightened young girl took hold of a tire swing...
4. A young boy ran as fast as he could...
5. A young bachelor sat at his desk and sighed...

Now, depending on what type of scene you would like to write—comedy, horror, fantasy, romance, etc., you can pick a song to accompany the type of genre you would like to write. For instance, if you would like to write a hero's journey, maybe film score music would be best, but if you want to write a present-day novel, current hip hop, rock, pop, or country may be best.

Choose one song that you believe fits the genre of what you are writing. Any song will do, and modify it if you need to.

As an example, if I picked "A young boy ran as fast as he could..." I could listen to film score music and come up with the following paragraph:

"A young boy ran as fast as he could toward the old stables by his father's cottage. He yanked the door open and found the Sword of Longhorn safely tucked away under a bale of hay. He took it into his hands and held it in front of him. He would defeat the dragon alone."

Or, I could use the same example and listen to a country song.

"A young boy ran as fast as he could toward his best friend. Up ahead, Ellie twirled around, laughing as she blew dandelion wishes into the sky, seemingly oblivious to what had just happened."

Once you have your song and you've set a scene with your example, it's time to engage the senses further. By listening to more music, you can build on the scene. Perhaps the boy in our first example runs to the stable in the pouring rain. He hears the snort of a horse, and the stable smells like damp rain and horse manure.

Now it's your turn. Pick one of the opening statements above, as well as an accompanying song, and see what you can come up with!

_____
_____
_____

Now, try this exercise with one of the ideas you have for your own book. Listen to a piece of music, and see how it shapes that idea. You might what to try this exercise a couple of times with different types of music.

Opening statement:_____
_____

Writing Exercise Day #15: Book Cover Brain Trick

"After you commit to writing a book, affirm that it is so, and put out strong output intentions, design your book cover, even if you haven't started the book yet."

CHAPTER SIX
OH, THE STORIES YOU WILL WRITE

Writing Exercise #15: Book Cover Brain Trick

Draw or use any free online template to make a rough cover of the book you would like to write. Print it out and prop it by your computer and look at it each time you write. Keep changing your cover as you become more and more involved with your book.

You can easily do this on websites like Canva.

If you are adept at Adobe Photoshop, you can use that.

You can even "draw" your cover. Use the blank cover below to sketch out a cover! Your name, title, etc. would go on the right-hand side. Don't forget to write your book blurb! The back of the book blurb would go on the left. Writing this blurb alone can significantly increase your book-writing momentum! I've also included just a "front cover" design on the next page. Don't forget to color it!

Remember, the more you see it, the more it becomes a reality for you.

Writing Exercise Day #16: Engaging the Senses

"Engaging all of our physical senses and beyond allows us to write the masterpiece we see in our minds!"

CHAPTER SIX
OH, THE STORIES YOU WILL WRITE

Writing Exercise #16: Engaging the Senses

Now, let's work on a small writing goal and try to either reach the number of words you set for today or exceed them. If you are describing a scene, don't forget to include all the senses of sights, smells, sounds, tastes, and touch. Is the wind blowing? Is the weather warm or cool? You don't have to write a masterpiece right now, as this is an exercise in getting started. If you are writing a character, what does he or she look like? What is he wearing? What other details do you want us to know about this character? If you are working on an experience, sit for a moment and instead of just focusing on the emotional aspect, try to remember all the sensory inputs around you at the time of the experience.

Writing Exercise Day #17: What's the Buzz?

*"A third way to trick the brain is to create a buzz about the book you're writing. Print out your cover, share with **supportive** family and friends, and even set a release date."*

CHAPTER SIX
OH, THE STORIES YOU WILL WRITE

Writing Exercise #17: What's the Buzz?

Create a pretend buzz about the book you are writing, even if you have not started a word of your book yet. Write phrases, statements, and paragraphs you would tell your close friends, family, or the internet world about your special project. Create a title for your project. Pick a release date and write it down. Even go as far as writing what types of formats you will release your book as a digital e-book, hardcover, paperback, audio-book, etc.

Affirm: *I am releasing (insert book title/writing project name) by (whatever date you choose).*
Example: *I am releasing A Death at the Speakeasy Inn by August 2024.*

You do not need all the details, but as you work on the project, revisit this exercise and continue to write more and more details or change certain ones until you are completely satisfied with the buzz you have written. When you are ready, take the leap and start creating the buzz out in the real world! Tell your friends, family, and the world that this project is on its way.

_____
_____
_____
_____
_____
_____
_____
_____
_____
_____
_____
_____
_____
_____
_____
_____
_____
_____
_____
_____
_____
_____

Writing Exercise Day #18: Current Status: Critical

"Criticizing ourselves and others is devastating to our self-esteem and can throw us into a perpetual loop of never truly feeling happiness and success. When we cut ourselves down, although we may justify this criticism as necessary for our improvement, we are actually showing the world that we do not believe in ourselves and that no one else should believe in us either."

CHAPTER SEVEN
OH, THE STORIES YOU WILL WRITE

Writing Exercise #18: Current Status: Critical

How many times do you criticize yourself in a day? Commit to a full day of being non-critical, not only to yourself but to others, especially those who know how to push your buttons *very* well. Use the chart below to write any limiting, critical thoughts that come into your mind during the day. Then examine these critical thoughts. Which ones are you willing to let go of?

Date	Critical Thought	Source (Me, or Someone Else)	Am I willing to let this go?

Write and repeat the following affirmation for each critical remark. Feel free to write it in your own words.

I am willing to let (whatever the critical remark is) go. The negative feelings of this criticism no longer serve me. I gain nothing from criticizing myself or others except more pain and unhappiness. Healthy self-esteem and true confidence is my only goal now. I know that others may criticize me because they are having self-esteem issues, and I send them love while I continue to focus on myself.

Try to go through each day and be mindful of how critical you are. Replace any negative, critical statements with positive ones instead.

Writing Exercise Day #19: Loveth Thy Selfeth

"We begin to "awaken" when we turn within and become aware of our limiting subconscious beliefs and conditioned patterns. We begin to feel inner confidence as we let limiting beliefs go, and we develop a love for the self through the realization that we are special, amazing, and wonderful regardless of our current external factors."

CHAPTER SEVEN
OH, THE STORIES YOU WILL WRITE

Writing Exercise #19: Loveth Thy Selfeth

List ten ways you could love yourself more.

Examples: *I could love myself more by praising my work more.*

I could love myself more by looking in the mirror and telling myself, "I love you."

Write down as many ways as you can think of how you can love yourself more. On a set of index cards write down *I love myself even though*...In the morning when you wake up, pick one thought about yourself.

I love myself, even though I did not pay my bill yesterday.

I love myself, even though I ate too many pieces of pizza. (Impossible!)

This exercise is a great way to determine subconscious beliefs you may be holding on to. With each "even though" belief, you can examine why you wrote it. As an example, if I love myself, even though I ate too many pieces of pizza, perhaps I was stress eating. There are many great authors, teachers, and therapists who talk about releasing limiting beliefs.

1. I could love myself more by
_____

2. I could love myself more by
_____

3. I could love myself more by
_____

4. I could love myself more by
_____

5. I could love myself more by
_____

6. I could love myself more by
_____

7. I could love myself more by
_____

8. I could love myself more by
_____

9. I could love myself more by
_____

10. I could love myself more by
_____

Writing Exercise Day #20: Call the Clutter Man!

"Keep your eye on the prize and your mind out of the clutter."

CHAPTER EIGHT
OH, THE STORIES YOU WILL WRITE

Writing Exercise #20: Call the Clutter Man!

Write down any negative or fear-based thoughts about writing, publishing, or anything else that is holding you back from success.

Fear-based thought #1:

Fear-based thought #2:

Fear-based thought #3:

Fear-based thought #4:

Fear-based thought #5:

Fear robs us of success and living a happy, healthy, joyful life. Sometimes we have to work extra hard to pull ourselves out of fear-based thoughts which keep us caged where we are instead of where we want to be. I've been through my fair share of these moments, especially after my mother's death. But what I have realized, and I hope you will also, is that fear is simply a state of mind. It is rarely reality. So, becoming aware of how these thoughts are robbing you of your happiness and success and then releasing them every time they pop into your mind is very helpful. I also teach my students that one way to overcome these fearful thoughts is through meditation (or, at the least, quieting the inner chatter that plagues most of us).

Ask yourself as you read your fear-based thought. Does this thought guide me toward my goals and success? Wholeness? Happiness? Joy? If the answer is no, then it's time to release the thought.

I am often reminded of the elephant tied to a rope story. It's a profound and sad little story about a baby elephant that is tied by a rope that will keep the elephant from running away. When the elephant gets bigger, the same little small rope is tied to it, but it will not run away. Why? Because it believes it can't. That is the elephant's state of mind. Whenever I have fear-based thoughts that keep me from growth and success, no matter if it's career, health, relationships, or more, I always think, this isn't the state of mind I want to stay in. There is freedom on the other side of fear.

Release your statements by affirming:

"I am in control of my thoughts. Because I believe in the concept of time, a past, and a future, I root myself in fear, worry, and pessimism based on what happened in the past and what may happen in the future. It is time for me to release these feelings. I release the thought of (insert negative or fear-based thought), and I replace it with a more empowering thought. Everything I think today will impact my life in the future."

Writing Exercise Day #21: Empower Yourself

"To achieve our dream, then, we must navigate through the thorns with persistence, knowing that we can clearly see the end goal or dream. We must believe that no matter how many thorns are in our path, we will eventually reach the castle if we push through hard enough."

CHAPTER EIGHT
OH, THE STORIES YOU WILL WRITE

Writing Exercise #21: Empower Yourself

Read or re-read the empowered mindset list from *Oh, the Stories You Will Write* (located at the end of this workbook for reference). Think about any areas on the list that you would like to improve in your life. Choose one and write down how you could improve that attitude. Take one action step each day toward improving it.

You would think that writing a book had nothing to do with some of these listed items, but I would argue that **action** only accounts for a portion of success. Truly successful people, first and foremost, have such an **empowered mindset** that there is no stopping them. They have the same failures and life issues as everyone else, but their success mindset is so strong they are able to "navigate through the thorns" and reach their end goals. When you have an empowered mindset, you are unstoppable, and that is what I have been guiding you to realize. Break free from the "normal." Don't let other people tell you who you can be and what you can accomplish. Don't even listen to yourself (if you happen to be stuck in a negative state of mind). *Be the CEO of your own success. You have it in you as much as anyone else!*

Here are a few examples:

Each day, I am going to take one action step toward my goal of writing a book.
    Action steps/Reflections:
    I set my word goal for 500 words a day.
    I created a character blueprint for one of my favorite characters.

I didn't meet my writing goal yesterday. I failed. Life is too difficult sometimes, and I can't get to writing.
    Action steps/Reflections:
    I set my word goal for 300 words for tomorrow.
    I am committed to writing this book and understand failure is just a stepping stone to success. I can use the feeling of disappointment inside me to catapult further into success tomorrow!

My friend told me I'm an amazing writer. But my other friend said she couldn't get into my writing.
    Action steps/Reflections:
    After meditating about this, I realize I am indifferent to both criticism and praise.
    I write because I realize my worth and value as a writer. That comes from within, not from without.

Area you would like to improve:

Action steps/Reflections:

Area you would like to improve:

Action steps/Reflections:

Area you would like to improve:

Action steps/Reflections:

2

A Deeper Dive into Developing Your Book

Bestseller Mapping Exercise Day #1: Getting Started

This exercise is one I came up with and used for my newest book series. It is incredibly helpful to stay motivated when writing a book. Sometimes the hardest part about writing a book is getting started. Over the years, I have also heard that if you want to be successful, study those who have been successful in the field you are pursuing. So, for this exercise, we will "map" or outline the first chapter of a bestselling book in the genre we are writing.

Before we do this, let's decide how you will choose the book you will map.

Here are a few suggestions.
1. Pick a book that has been on the bestseller list in the genre that you plan on writing. This may be a non-fiction memoir, a children's picture book, adult fiction, self-help, romance, YA fiction, teen fiction, and more. Narrow down your larger genre and then your more focused one, such as YA Mystery or Adult Romance.

2. The book you pick does not have to be published by a major publisher. We would like to think that all the books published by the largest publishing companies that are on the bestselling list are the best of the best; however, sometimes, that is simply not the case. Publishing companies, first and foremost, are a business of profit. A bestselling celebrity memoir from a major publishing company is not necessarily the best memoir written by the best author. It is, however, the most marketable to that company, and therefore, they will go to great lengths to get it on the bestseller list. The celebrity's name is part of that process. A bestseller from an author who is not well-established or who is not a celebrity is where you want to look. These authors may be published by a major publishing company, a small publishing company, or an independent publishing company. They may even be self-published or republished after being self-published.

3. The purpose of this exercise is to stimulate your imagination with regard to your book idea, so take your time going through the process.

4. If one book isn't lighting the match for you, move on to the next. There is a plethora of books to choose from.

5. You can pick a book that you know, but I can promise you that you will have more fun with this exercise reading a book you do not know.

6. Even though you may be writing a sequel, I would not recommend reading a sequel for this exercise.

The exercise for today is to read the first few pages of this book. You can read the prologue or introduction, but you will not be using those parts of the book for this exercise. Focus on the first chapter, the first few pages. When you've finished, move on to the next exercise.

Bestseller Mapping Exercise Day #2: Let's Set the Scene

Map or outline the first chapter. Start with the first scene.

- For fiction and non-fiction books: Is the first scene enticing? Does it draw you in? (If not, pick a different book!)
- **For fiction books:** What is happening in this first scene? What characters are introduced? What are they doing in the first scene? What are some of the sights, sounds, and smells described in the scene?
- **For non-fiction books:** What exactly drew you into the first scene? For self-help, let's say, what are some of the themes or lessons of the book that keep you reading? For memoirs, what are the sights, sounds, and smells described in the scene? Regardless of genre, how has the author's writing grabbed you?

_____
_____
_____
_____
_____
_____
_____
_____
_____
_____
_____
_____
_____
_____
_____
_____
_____
_____

Bestseller Mapping Exercise Day #3: Diving Deeper

Read a few more pages of the first chapter of the bestselling book you are mapping and answer the following questions. **(Please note: You may not be able to answer all of these questions depending on the genre of the book you are reading.)**

For fiction books:

- What happens next?
- Are any new characters introduced?
- Are any new storylines introduced that may have an impact later?
- What is the scenery of the book like? Do you have a clear picture of it?
- What kinds of words does the author use to describe his or her scenery?
- What are the characters like? What kinds of words does the author use to describe the main characters?
- How did scene one flow into scene two? What specifically did you notice about the flow from scene one to scene two?

For non-fiction books:

- How has the author kept your interest in the next few pages? Is it the content? Writing style? Humor? Description?
- How is the content presented? Is it fact by fact or told in a story form?
- Has the author used his or her story to draw you along?
- If the book is about the author or someone else, how does he describe this person? What draws you to the author's story?

_____
_____
_____
_____
_____

Bestseller Mapping Exercise Day #4: Getting to the Finish Line

- A main chapter may have more or less than three scenes, so fit these exercises to match the book you picked.
- If your book has more than three scenes, then continue to map the book as you did with the last exercise. If this is the last scene, then you can proceed with this one.
- Read the rest of the first chapter and analyze the last scene.

For Fiction Books:

- How did the author end the first chapter of the book? Did she leave it as a cliffhanger? Do you want to read more?
- Did anything about the end of the first chapter allude to what may happen in further chapters?
- Are there any mysterious characters or storylines that the author weaves in that you are interested in learning more about?

For Non-Fiction Books:

- How did the author end the first chapter?
- What kept you wanting to read the next chapter?
- How does the layout of this first chapter set this book up for success?

_____
_____
_____
_____
_____
_____
_____
_____
_____

Bestseller Mapping Exercise Day #5: Applying This Process To Your Work

Now that you have taken the time to do this exercise, it's time to think about your own story and apply the research you have gathered. From my observations, while the stories, plot lines, characters, scenes, ideas, and themes may differ, most bestsellers in a particular genre follow a *pattern* or *formula*. Figure out the pattern and apply it to your work! Have you been able to figure out what your genre's formula is? Perhaps it's the heroic journey of the main character or engaging stories from people around the world. Considering small goals, think about how you might use the "formula" of the specific genre you wish to write in order to introduce your own story. How might you match the level of engagement of the bestseller you chose when introducing your ideas?

Let's say, for instance, you are writing a memoir. Thinking about the scope of the story you are about to tell, what might be an engaging opening scene? Is it a wedding? A birth? A death?

Or, if you're writing a fiction book, think about one of the important settings of your book. Let's say you are writing a book that takes place at the beach. How might you introduce your main character(s) in a way that captivates your audience based on the work you did mapping a bestseller? What might be happening in the opening scene that makes your readers want to read more?

If you are writing a self-help book, maybe you want to use your own personal story to draw others into the book.

Take some time to work with this exercise, but don't let it overwhelm you. If nothing comes to you, focus on creating small scenes or chapters that follow the formula. Then you can come back to the opening chapter when you're ready.

_____
_____
_____
_____
_____
_____
_____
_____
_____

Keypoints about Mapping a Bestseller

1. From my observations, while the stories, plot lines, characters, scenes, ideas, and themes may differ, most bestsellers in a particular genre follow a pattern or formula. Figure out the pattern and apply it to your work!

2. If you "map" the formula throughout the book, you will find a harmonious flow of enticing scenes that keep you reading until the end, regardless of whether or not the book is fiction or non-fiction.

3. Remember that if you struggle with this exercise, pick another book! You can always go to your local library and reserve books for free.

4. At the least, this exercise is meant to stimulate your imagination. I can't tell you how many times I would put the book I was reading down throughout this process because original creative ideas popped into my head, and I had to write them down!

5. Remember to consider small goals when writing. It will help alleviate some of the anxiety and pressure of writing the book!

6. If you can work on the opening scene, great. If not, simply work on a scene that calls to you.

7. Reread a chapter if you still can't find the formula. Especially when you get toward the end of a chapter, look for the transitions, as they are what typically keep people reading.

3

Worksheets to Keep Writing Momentum

Word Goal Log

Day/Date	Word Goal	Words Written	Writing Time

Small Writing Goal To-Do List

✓ when complete

Week Of _____

☐ **Small Writing Goal:** _____

_____

Projected amount of time you will dedicate to this task: _____

☐ **Small Writing Goal:** _____

_____

Projected amount of time you will dedicate to this task: _____

☐ **Small Writing Goal:** _____

_____

Projected amount of time you will dedicate to this task: _____

☐ **Small Writing Goal:** _____

_____

Projected amount of time you will dedicate to this task: _____

☐ **Small Writing Goal:** _____

_____

Projected amount of time you will dedicate to this task: _____

☐ **Small Writing Goal:** _____

_____

Projected amount of time you will dedicate to this task: _____

Twelve Tips for Writing Success

Tip One:
Building momentum in the direction of our dreams is a leading factor of success.

Tip Two:
Become a LEAPER.

Tip Three:
The stronger your intention is for writing, the stronger your attention will be on your goal and the easier it will be to write your story.

Tip Four:
Allot time for writing, log your word count, and develop your writing skills.

Tip Five:
If you cannot find the "right" words, say anything by SIMPLIFYING THE STATEMENT.

Tip Six:
Physical expressions of emotion and states of being are more powerful than words.

Tip Seven:
Discover your best habits for unleashing your creativity.

Tip Eight:
Use positive tools and practices that resonate with you to help stimulate your creative mind.

Tip Nine:
Engaging all of our physical senses and beyond allows us to write the masterpiece we see in our minds!

Tip Ten:
Create your book cover as soon as you commit to writing a book.

Tip Eleven:
Build a confident, indestructible infrastructure.

Tip Twelve:
The empowered mindset gets the gold.

The Empowered Mindset

1. *You do not rely on external factors for happiness. Happiness comes from within. You understand that external happiness and pleasure are fleeting and do not last. You understand that finding internal, lasting happiness comes from awareness of ego, the false "conditioned" self, letting go and releasing conditioned, limiting beliefs, following true purpose, helping others (animals, plants, and people), and engaging in activities that bring you pure joy.*
2. *You know what you want and take one step/action toward your dream each day.*
3. *You recognize and understand the conditioning of the brain and work each day to release old programming and create new subconscious beliefs.*
4. *You realize all beliefs are conditioned and attachment to negative beliefs can bring pain and lack of growth. You are open to new ideas and ways of thinking without reacting to new ideas from a place of attachment.*
5. *You use intuition or a "gut feeling" to know if something is right for you.*
6. *You are happy with yourself and lift others with your inner confidence.*
7. *You know that criticism and negativity only bring more unhappiness. The more negative energy you create and intertwine with, the more negative circumstances you experience.*
8. *You do not believe in the word "failure." In fact, the definition of "failure" for you is that it is only a minor obstacle that, when confronted, will only make you better and stronger.*
9. *You take leaps when it is necessary and take calculated risks when dealing with money or important life situations. You refrain from hesitation unless hard facts or intuition, not ego, tell you to hold off.*
10. *You are indifferent to praise and criticism. Your inner confidence is indestructible enough that no one's words affect you. You are kind to yourself and others and go about your days, knowing that your choices are making you happy. Those who try to bring you down no longer deserve your company. Still, you send them love. You do all you can to help those in need, but not at the expense of other people draining your energy. You understand that everyone's journey is personal and while you try to inspire others, you do not push others unless they want to change. You choose to spend time with those who lift your energy, and in turn, you lift theirs also.*
11. *You understand that once you master the mind, you can master anything.*

A Guide to Confidence Building

~A Summary~

1. Refrain from criticizing yourself and others. Be kind to yourself and praise yourself for doing something others feel is impossible.
2. Associate with people who motivate and lift you and politely decline those who constantly put themselves (and the industry) in a negative light.
3. Recognize that negative criticism toward you is more a reflection of the unhappiness and insecurity of the person doing the criticism than of your weaknesses.
4. Build self-esteem through reading books about self-esteem.
5. Even if you make a huge mistake, do not judge yourself. Simply see the lesson and opportunity to grow within that mistake and keep moving.
6. Tune into your internal "current best" meter and give any project you are working on your all. Produce at your *current* best. Learn and improve. Produce at your new current best. If you know you can do something better than the first time you did it, simply say, "I did my very best, and that is all that matters. It is more important for me to complete projects and then assess if I can make them better than not to complete them at all because I want them to be so perfect." As Voltaire, the French writer said, "The best is the enemy of the good."
7. Do not measure your self-worth by the "things" you have accumulated or the accolades you have received. Inner confidence is indifferent to accolades and criticisms.
8. Never ever put yourself down.

FINAL THOUGHTS

I hope you have found value in this workbook and continue to use it as you write the book you have always wanted to write. I truly believe you have the ability to write, even if in the past you felt you did not.

To the authors who have found the courage, motivation, stamina, and drive to finish their books with the guidance and help of my tools, I commend you, and I look forward to reading your work!

I want to hear from you!

If you have felt inspired by this book, please email me at stefanimilanauthor@gmail.com and tell me your story!

All the best,
Stefani Milan

ACKNOWLEDGMENTS

This workbook came about with the help of some important people I am lucky to call friends.

First, thank you to Carol Harkavy, my author friend and writing partner. I am so thankful to have you as part of my writing tribe. Your enthusiasm, ambition, and dedication to your work match my own and inspire me daily to keep doing my work. Thank you for reading this workbook and making important editing suggestions. You are indeed a light and wonderful friend in my life!

Thank you to Anna Marie Hrivnak, another wonderful author friend and member of my writing tribe, for always giving me wise insight on where to go next with my books. The many parts of this workbook came about after taking your highly respected advice.

A special thanks to my husband, Jon, who continues to support my writing career and cheer me on with each book I complete.

Lastly, thank you to the many writers I have met over the years who inspired this workbook. To quote Rose (Rosie) Anderman from Carol Harkavy's *Vignettes on Life: Reflections of a Septuagenarian*, "I've got my money on you!"

ABOUT THE AUTHOR

With over seven published books under the pseudonyms Stefani Milan and R.A. Milan, Stefani has spent ten years navigating the ever-changing field of self-publishing. In addition to writing, she spends her time coaching aspiring writers to complete their projects and helping them to self-publish their works.

Stefani received her Bachelor's Degree in English from Rutgers University Camden. She has been a licensed skincare therapist for the last sixteen years, has a Reiki Certification, and was certified in Nutrition and Healthy Living through Cornell University. In addition, she teaches balanced living with her certification as a Chopra Health Instructor and is currently finishing a new book that explores the links between higher-consciousness and creative writing, specifically through the lens of Ayurveda.

She lives in Southern New Jersey with her husband, sons, and animals (many of which are rescued cats).

MORE BY MILAN BOOK PUBLISHING

Children's Fiction
I Liked You Much Better When You Were Outside by Stefani Milan
I Think I Like You, Cat by Stefani Milan
If I Were a Cat by Stefani Milan

Children's Educational Books
The Land of the Past: Teaching Past Tense Book One by Lauren Milanese and Stefani Milan

Memoir
This Side of the Dream by Stefani Milan
Vignettes on Life: Reflections of a Septuagenarian by Carol Harkavy

Fiction
The Secret of Kolney Hatch by R. A. Milan
Kolney Hatch: Green with Envy by R.A. Milan

Creativity/Self-Help
Oh, the Stories You Will Write: A Motivational Guide to Empower Aspiring Authors by Stefani Milan

Coming Soon!
A Death at the Speakeasy Inn by R.A. Milan

www.ingramcontent.com/pod-product-compliance
Lightning Source LLC
Chambersburg PA
CBHW060425010526
44118CB00017B/2369